MARK McGWIRE

★

CHIPPER JONES

Also by East End Publishing, Ltd.

BASKETBALL SUPERSTARS ALBUM 1996
MICHAEL JORDAN * MAGIC JOHNSON
ANFERNEE HARDAWAY * GRANT HILL
SHAQUILLE O'NEAL * LARRY JOHNSON
PRO FOOTBALL'S ALL-TIME ALL-STAR TEAM
STEVE YOUNG * JERRY RICE
TROY AIKMAN * STEVE YOUNG
GRED MADDUX * CAL RIPKIN JR.
KEN GRIFFEY JR. * FRANK THOMAS
BOBBY BONDS * ROBERTO ALOMAR
MARIO LEMIEUX
THE WORLD SERIES: THE GREAT CONTESTS
TOUCHDOWN! THE FOOTBALL FUN BOOK
MICHAEL JORDAN
GRANT HILL
SHAQUILLE O'NEAL
WAYNE GRETZKY

For more information on how to order these exciting sports books, see the back pages of this book.

MARK McGWIRE

★

CHIPPER JONES

JON D. GELBERG

EAST END PUBLISHING, LTD.
SYOSSET, NY

This book is dedicated to my family—the people who have put up with me as I've traveled from city to city, from game to game:

To my wife, Debra, my best friend.

To my son, Michael, who provided me with a kid's perspective and a child's wisdom as he read, then fixed, my manuscript.

To my son, Robbie, whose hugs and laughter were always a welcome distraction as I plowed my way through the pages.

To my parents who gave me the greatest gift of all, a love of words, of books, of ideas.

Special thanks are in order for my editor, Richard J. Brenner, who put this whole thing together, from conception through completion.

MARK MCGWIRE * CHIPPER JONES
First Printing January, 1997   ISBN: 0-9433403-3-X

The cover photos were snapped by Tony Inzerillo.
Cover design by Jim Wasserman.
Copyright 1997 by Richard Brenner – East End Publishing, Ltd.

Cataloging-in-Publication Data

920   Gelberg, Jon D. (Jon David), 1957 Feb. 14-
GEL   Mark McGwire * Chipper Jones / Jon D. Gelberg. - Syosset, NY: East End Publishing, Ltd., ©1997

96 p: ill. : 18 cm.

Summary: A dual biography of two of professional baseball's superstars, Mark McGwire, first baseman for the Oakland A's, and Atlanta Braves third baseman Chipper Jones.

ISBN: 0-943403-43-X

1. McGwire, Mark - Juveniles literature   2. Jones, Chipper- Juvenile literature 3. Baseball players - United States - Biography - Juvenile literature I. Title

GVS65   920; [B] ; 796.357092_dc20

Provided in cooperation with Unique Books, Inc.

Contents

MARK McGWIRE

1. The Kid's a Hit

[Author's Note: In this book, there are numerous references to teams with Native–American inspired names, like the "Atlanta Braves" and the "Cleveland Indians."

Some people find such names to be racist or inappropriate. It is an issue that Major League Baseball and other professional and college sports teams are dealing with at this very moment. If you have strong feelings, one way or another, please contact the Office of the Commissioner of Baseball or the teams themselves. The addresses can be found on page 91of this book.]

Mark McGwire was nervous. Real nervous. It was 1973, and Mark was ten years old and playing in his first Little League game.

When you're playing in your first organized game, you can't be sure whether you're any good or not. Mark would find out in a hurry.

He walked up to the plate, settled into the batter's box, and took a deep breath. The pitcher stared at his catcher, got the sign, then took a quick glance at Mark. He went into his windup and fired a fastball.

Mark swung as hard as he could. The bat met the ball squarely, sending it arching high into the sky.

The right fielder went back, all the way to the fence, where the sign read 175 feet. He stuck up his glove, but could only look on helplessly as the ball flew over the fence.

As Mark circled the bases, he allowed himself a little smile. So *this* is what it feels like to hit a home run. It was the best feeling he had ever had. At that moment, he had no idea how many times he would have that feeling again.

On this day, he hit a home run in front of a group of family, friends, and neighbors. One day, he'd be hitting them in stadiums packed with 50,000 cheering fans.

More than 20 years have passed since that first home run. Since then, Mark has hit hundreds of them—first in Little League, then in high school and college, then in the Olympics, and, now, with the Oakland A's. Along the way, there have been hundreds of outfielders who have shared the fate of watching helplessly as Mark's homers fly over the fence.

Mark McGwire was born on October 1, 1963 in Pomona, California, an upper-middle-class suburb of Los Angeles. The McGwires had everything money could buy, including a nice house, plenty of clothes, and all the sports equipment they could ever want.

Alhough his family was prosperous, Mark was never spoiled. Mark and his four brothers were expected to work hard in all things they did, whether it was working on a science project or playing Little League baseball.

The McGwire kids didn't need any pushing when it came to playing ball, however. Almost from the time they could walk, the boys played everything, from baseball to football to basketball. They even played golf.

Mark credits his parents, John and Ginger, with instilling a love of sports. Mark's father was his primary role model. John had battled back from polio, a crippling disease contracted when he was only seven years old, to lead a normal life. Alhough he had to walk with a cane, the disability hardly slowed him down. A practicing dentist, John McGwire had been an amateur boxer and was an excellent golfer. He once even rode a bicycle from San Francisco, in northern California, all the way to San Diego, at the southern tip of the state, a distance of more than 500 miles.

Despite his physical limitations, John always got involved in his sons' activities. He coached Mark and his brothers in Little League and taught them how to play golf.

Ginger, Mark's mother, was also a major influence on the

10

McGwire boys. If the kids had to be at a game, she'd always be there to take them. If they needed a friendly face in the crowd, they could always look up and see her cheering them on.

"I've always assumed we were like most families," said Ginger, who swam competitively while in college. "We tried to teach our kids the importance of always doing their best, being polite, and respecting other people."

With five boys running around the house, things were never quiet in the McGwire household. At any given time, the five boys could be found playing five different sports. All of them grew to be at least 6-2, and at least 215 pounds. Dan, one of Mark's younger brothers, grew to be the tallest, at 6-8; he went on to become a professional football player, drafted out of San Diego State in the first round of the 1991 National Football league draft by the Seattle Seahawks.

Getting the whole family to sit down at the dinner table was almost impossible. Feeding them was even harder. "It was amazing how much food was eaten in our house," Mark recalled. "My mom used to spend $200 twice a week at the supermarket. She really had trouble keeping the refrigerator full. When she was cooking, she had to double or triple every recipe."

Alhough he was always one of the biggest kids in his class, Mark was never a bully. In fact, he was one of the quietest children in school. "I was always the kind of kid who liked to sit in the back of the room and blend in," he said.

By the time he was eight years old, though, Mark knew that he would have to wear glasses if he wanted to see the blackboard from the back row. "I have the worst eyes you can possibly have. No lie. Without glasses, I can't even see the Big E on the eye chart."

Luckily for Mark, his weak eyes were more than offset by a large, strong, and agile body that allowed him to excel athletically. On the diamond, Mark started showing what he could do at the plate in his first Little League game. But, for a long time, he got a bigger kick overpowering overmatched batters with his high-velocity fastball than he did in teeing off against opposing pitchers. Instead of being boastful about his abilities, however, Mark tends to downplay them. "I was always just a basic athlete, nothing extraordinary," he insists.

Although Mark loved baseball and clearly had a gift for the game, his favorite sport early in life was golf. His father showed him how to hold a golf club when he was just five years old, and it was love at first swing. During his sophomore year of high school, Mark even quit baseball to concentrate on golf. "Golf was really the first game I learned," Mark said. "The thing I liked about golf was that you were the only one to blame when something went wrong."

As much as he loved golf, however, Mark found the game to be a little boring when he began playing it all the time. So, Mark decided to switch his focus back to baseball, the sport that provided the type of excitement he preferred.

Once Mark rededicated himself to baseball, he went at it non-stop. Not content to coast along on his natural talent, Mark was constantly striving to improve both his hitting and his pitching. "I was a hard worker," recalled Mark. "I'd throw balls against a cement wall or set a ball on a tee so I could work on my swing."

The work paid off. He dominated his league while playing for Damien High School. Pretty soon, professional and college scouts were dropping by to see his games.

When his senior year of high school came to an end, Mark wasn't sure whether he wanted to go right to professional baseball or to go to college instead. The Montreal Expos, though, were betting that Mark would go pro, so they used their first pick in the 1981 Amateur Draft—the No. 8 pick overall—to select Mark. When it came time to discuss dollars, however, it soon became clear that Montreal didn't want to pay Mark very much money. "If the Expos don't think I'm worth much," Mark figured, "then I'll wait until some other team decides I am."

In the meantime, Mark decided that he would go to college,

where he could play baseball and further his education. One of the schools that had a lot of interest in him was the University of Southern California, a college that, traditionally, fields one of the best college nines in the country. The head coach at USC, Rod Dedeaux, sent his pitching coach, Marcel Lachemann, to get a close look at Mark. "I saw him pitch three games," recalled Lachemann. "In all three, he hit two home runs. I told Rod that Mark had a great arm, but he also had the potential to be an outstanding power hitter."

The USC coaching staff was excited about Mark's dual potential as a pitcher and a hitter, so Lachemann went to the McGwire home to sell the family on the great opportunities and traditions at USC. He mentioned Hall of Famer Tom Seaver, a former Trojan star who had gone on to win three Cy Young Awards between 1969 and 1975 while pitching for the New York Mets. Lachemann also spoke about Dave Kingman, who had also worn USC's burgundy-and-gold uniform before he went on to become one of the major league's top home run hitters from 1971 through 1986.

Mark liked what he heard, so he shook hands with Lachemann, and the deal was done. But Mark had an uneasy feeling in the pit of his stomach. Did he have doubts about his decision? Should he have gone with the Expos instead?

Actually, the feeling in his stomach was a bad case of appendicitis. The morning after he agreed to go to USC, Mark was in the hospital undergoing an appendectomy. Lying in the hospital, all Mark could think about was the last thing he had eaten, his mother's strawberry pie. He hasn't tried a strawberry since.

14

2. USC Slugger

As soon as Mark arrived at USC, he realized that he had made the right decision. He enjoyed college life: the classes, his new friends, and, of course, baseball.

Because USC is located in Los Angeles, Mark could practice and play baseball year-round. In addition to favorable weather, the school had terrific facilities and great coaches, and played a schedule that took the baseball team all over the country.

Mark found that competition at the collegiate level was much tougher than anything he had faced in high school. As a freshman, he went 4–4, with an earned run average of 3.04. College hitters, he found, could hit his fastball a lot better than high school hitters could. He still dreamed of pitching in the major leagues, but realized that it wouldn't be as easy as he had assumed.

Although Mark spent most of his time working with Dedeaux and Lachemann, it was the team's hitting instructor, Ron Vaughn, who took a special interest in him. Vaughn looked at Mark's size, his massive forearms (some of his teammates called him "Popeye" because his forearms were so huge), and his sheer strength and knew that he was looking at a kid with the potential to be a big-time power hitter.

Vaughn, who coached during the summers in Alaska, asked Mark whether he wanted to go to Anchorage after the spring semester and play for the Glacier Pilots. The great thing about Alaska, Vaughn explained, was that it was light almost 24 hours a day during the summer. There would be plenty of time to play and practice.

The two worked closely that summer, and Mark really concentrated on hitting techniques for the first time in his life. Because hitting had always come naturally to him, he had never worked on the fundamentals. "That summer was the first time I really ever took hitting seriously," Mark said. "I owe a lot to Ron Vaughn. He taught me how to stand, hold the bat, and hit the ball. I never had any kind of idols as a kid, but Ron is kind of my idol. He is like a personal coach to me."

The work in Alaska certainly paid off. When Mark returned to school for his sophomore year, he set a new school record by hitting 19 home runs.

Mark continued to pitch his sophomore year, going 3–1 in limited duty. But, although he was one of the best pitchers on the team, it was already clear that his future was going to be with his bat, not his arm.

"It was a tough decision for Mark because he had always thought of himself as a pitcher," Dedeaux said. "But Mark is such a competitor that he wanted to be in the lineup regularly." Mark was moved to first base, and that's the position he's continued to play throughout his baseball career.

In his junior year, he really blossomed as a hitter by blasting 32 balls over the fence. His remarkable output not only shattered the single-season record that he had set as a sophomore, it also equaled what had been USC's *career* home run record. Mark made it look so easy that the school decided to push the fences back by 20 feet after that record-breaking season. And Mark wasn't just hitting for power. He finished his junior season with a batting average of .378, a testament both to Vaughn's teaching and Mark's hard work.

Mark had another reason to celebrate during his junior year, because he married Kathy, a fellow USC student and bat girl for the baseball team. The added financial responsibilities of marriage, however, caused Mark to decide that the time had come to quit college and become a professional baseball player.

The Oakland A's, who had the No. 10 pick in the 1984 Amateur Draft, never dreamed that Mark would still be available when it was their turn. The Mets, who had the first pick in the draft, were very interested in taking Mark. But, having seen how the Expos had been stung three years earlier, they wanted to be absolutely sure they could sign Mark before risking the No. 1 pick on him. Mark, in fact, did turn down the Mets' predraft offer, so they wound up spending their selection on Shawn Abner, a heavy-hitting prep star who never fulfilled his big-league promise. It was a mistake they still regret.

The A's kept their fingers crossed as team after team decided to take other players. Finally, at the No. 10 pick, the A's grabbed him.

Before Mark signed his first pro contract, he seized the opportunity of a lifetime by earning a spot on the United States Olympic baseball team. Even though baseball was still only a demonstration sport at the 1984 games, Mark was thrilled to be representing his country. Mark was especially excited because the Olympics were being held in Los Angeles. His family and friends would therefore be able to watch him play and share the experience with him.

With Cuba, a baseball powerhouse, boycotting the Olympics for political reasons, the United States became the heavy favorite to win the tournament. The U.S. team, which featured future major league all-stars Will Clark, B.J. Surhoff, and Barry Larkin, breezed through the first round of the Olympic tournament, winning all three games by a combined 30 –2 margin.

The U.S. squad continued on its winning ways with a 5–2 victory over the Korean team in the semifinals. The U.S. had to settle for the silver medal, however, when it was upset, 6–3, in the finals by the Japanese team.

Mark was disappointed by his own poor performance, which consisted of only four singles in 21 at-bats. But, he was even more shocked that the U.S. team hadn't won the gold medal. To this day, Mark can't believe that the U.S. didn't beat Japan as it had in pre-Olympic games. "That might have been the best amateur team that was ever put together," Mark recalled. "I mean, Barry Larkin hardly got to play on that team."

17

3. Rookie of the Year

With the disappointment of the Olympics behind him, it was time for Mark to go to "work." A professional now, Mark had to make his way through the A's minor league system. Even though he had been one of the greatest players in the history of college baseball, Mark had to start proving himself, all over again.

The minor leagues have several levels, beginning with instructional leagues, then going through Single-A, Double-A and Triple-A. Many players never even get past the Single-A level.

The first brief stop for Mark was with the Single-A Modesto A's of the California League, a team for which he hit a modest .200 in 55 plate appearances.

The following year, in Mark's first full season in the minors, he returned to Modesto and began to show the power that would make him one of the most feared hitters in all of baseball. He whacked 23 homers and 23 doubles, topped the circuit with 106 runs, batted in, and was named the California League's Rookie of the Year.

The next year, Mark was promoted to AA ball, playing for the Huntsville, Alabama A's. In 55 games with Huntsville, Mark hit .303, with 10 homers and 53 runs batted in. Those numbers earned him a midseason promotion to the A's Triple-A farm club in Tacoma, Washington. But Triple-A pitchers had no more luck against Mark than their Double-A counterparts. In 78 games in Tacoma, Mark hit .318, with 13 homers and 59 RBIs.

Mark's only problem in the minors was his fielding. The A's wanted to see whether he could play third base, but Mark struggled at the hot corner, making 41 errors in his final minor league season.

Tony LaRussa, then manager of the Oakland A's, kept hearing great things about Mark. He didn't like rushing young players to the major leagues, but Mark didn't give him much of a choice. He was just too good to be in the minors.

Finally, on August 20, Mark received his call-up to the Big Show. Instead of walking into the A's clubhouse like a conquering hero, however, he stood and stared at the names above the locker stalls. He saw former USC star Dave Kingman, as well as future Hall of Famer Reggie Jackson and Jose Canseco, who was ripping up American League pitching on his way to earning Rookie of the Year honors.

On August 24, Mark stroked his first major league hit, a single off former New York Yankees ace Tommy John. When Mark was growing up, he had idolized John, who was, by great coincidence, a dental patient of Mark's dad. Two days later, Mark slugged his first big league homer, a towering 440-foot drive to straightaway center field off Walt Terrell, who was hurling for the Detroit Tigers.

These two hits were the highlights in what was, for Mark, an otherwise disappointing introduction to life in the big leagues. In trying so hard to please, he constantly overswung and wound up batting only .189, with ten hits and three homers in 53 at-bats. Mark also had problems in the field. He made six errors while playing at third base, a position at which he never really felt comfortable. Mark had discovered that the jump from the minor leagues to the major leagues is even more difficult than the leap from high school to college ball.

After a long, anxious winter, Mark was invited back to the A's spring training in Phoenix, Arizona. The A's, though, weren't sure where to put him. They played him some at third base, where he struggled, at first base, and in the outfield. LaRussa was trying to solve a problem caused by the fact that his two best rookie prospects, Mark and Rob Nelson, were both natural first basemen.

Mark and Nelson began the season platooning, taking turns playing first base. It was a situation that left neither player happy. When you have two players fighting for the same job, there's pressure on every at-bat, every play in the field.

Neither man responded well to the situation. Nelson ended up losing the job by striking out in 12 of his 24 trips to the plate. On April 20, LaRussa decided to send Nelson down to the minors and give Mark the first base job. Mark felt very fortunate, because he was hitting only .169 at the time. "Mac was swinging the bat better than Nelson," LaRussa explained. "But neither guy was hitting at all."

Year's later, LaRussa admitted it was one of the luckiest decisions of his life. "It wasn't like I was sure that Mark was going to turn out to be a great hitter," he said. "Managers have to make these decisions all the time—deciding who stays and who goes. I'm glad I made the decision to go with Mark."

The one thing LaRussa loved about Mark was his work ethic. Even when he wasn't playing well, Mark was always the hardest worker on the team. "He was something to see," LaRussa said. "He hit off the tee, in batting practice, in intrasquad games, in exhibitions. He hit in every situation possible. We had to find a position for him."

Ironically, LaRussa never actually told Mark that he was the starting first baseman; it just kind of happened. "He never told me, point-blank," Mark recalled. "Maybe they didn't want me to think it was mine, and I realize if I don't produce, it won't be. But that was a real turning point for me."

Once he knew that he was not only a member of the A's, but the starting first baseman, Mark could relax and focus all of his attention on playing the game. The results were instantaneous. After hitting only four homers in April, Mark caught fire in May, hitting, remarkably, 15 homers, just one shy of Mickey Mantle's major league record for May.

Seemingly overnight, Mark McGwire became a household name. Although he was only 23, Mark was being compared with the greatest home run hitters in baseball history.

Finally, Mark felt like he really belonged in the majors. "The game is a lot easier when you come to the park every day knowing you're going to play," he said. "The great thing about being an everyday ballplayer is you don't have to make a season in a week or a month. "You make a season in a season.' And what a season it would turn out to be.

By the All-Star break, Mark had 33 home runs and 68 RBIs. These weren't just great numbers for a rookie, they were some of the biggest halfseason numbers put up by anyone in baseball history. After only three months as a major leaguer, Mark was already being compared with Roger Maris, who broke Babe Ruth's single-season record by hitting 61 homers in 1961.

By August 11, Mark had tied the rookie home run record (held by Frank Robinson and Wally Berger), hitting his 38th. Three days later, he hit his 39th, off Don Sutton, and had set his own standard. It wasn't just that he was hitting homers, he was hitting homers further than anybody else in the game.

Mark's teammate Reggie Jackson was also known for his prodigious homers. When Jackson hit a long homer, he'd stand at home plate, admire the hit, then slowly, very slowly, trot around the bases. When Mark hit one, he just put his head down, ran hard to first base, and kept running until he was home. "Son, when you hit one like that, you've got to watch it," Jackson told Mark after one of his monster shots.

"No," Mark replied. "That's not my style."

They may have circled the bases at different speeds, but Jackson was still impressed with Mark's ability. "Mark McGwire is for real," Jackson said. "He has that swing that drives the ball, a good full cut. His swing isn't compact, but it's controlled. He's a fly-ball hitter, but his fly balls go 410 feet. When he hits the ball good, it goes 450 feet. When he hits them you never wonder whether it's going to be a home run."

As the season went on, Mark got closer and closer to the 50–home run mark. As the homers piled on, though, so did the media attention. Not a day went by when someone didn't ask him about breaking Maris's record. Every city he went to, there were reporters asking the same questions, over and over again.

Mark, who was basically shy, had trouble dealing with the all of the attention. He went to one press conference in New York, expecting to meet with one or two reporters. His jaw dropped when he found himself in a room with about 40 reporters and a dozen television cameras.

With one day left in the season, Mark had 49 homers. He was two homers up on George Bell for the American League home run title and was tied with Andre Dawson of the Chicago Cubs for the Major League lead.

The night before the final game, the phone rang in Mark's hotel room in Chicago. It was his wife Kathy, and she was about to have a baby.

For most people, this would have been an agonizing decision. At the time, only a dozen players in baseball history had ever hit 50 homers. How many people would pass up such a chance? Mark, though, didn't even think twice. There was no way he was going to miss the birth of his first child, even if it meant missing out on 50 homers.

After a frenzied trip to the airport, then to the hospital, Mark arrived just in time for the birth of his son, Matt.

The next day, a friend told Mark that the wind had been blowing out to straightaway center field at Chicago's Comisky Park. It had been a perfect day to hit a home run. "I've never had any regrets," he said. "There would be other chances for 50 homers, but never another first born.

"I've come to terms with it. I'm realistic. I don't know that I'll ever hit 49 home runs again. If I do, great. All I want to do is perform well and have some fun."

When his rookie season came to an end, Mark realized just how tough it had been on him and his family. Standing in the spotlight is simply not the place for a shy person. He didn't like giving interviews. He was overwhelmed by the attention he was getting from fans.

"I still can't believe what I did this year," said Mark, who was named American League Rookie of the Year, becoming only the seventh player in the history of the award to earn a unanimous selection. "But it really took a toll on me. Players who have played for 15 years haven't had to deal with what I dealt with. I never wanted to be in the public eye. I can't even go into a restaurant without being bothered. Everybody knows me as Mark McGwire the baseball player. I don't want to be just the baseball player. I want to be myself."

4. The World Series Years

It would be a long time before Mark could match the individual heroics of his rookie season. In fact, it would be nine years before he would match the huge numbers he posted in 1987.

From 1988 through 1990, Mark's individual achievements took a back seat to the success of his team. In those three years, the A's dominated baseball, winning a total of 306 regular-season games, three straight pennants, and one World Series.

Those Oakland teams were built on a combination of great pitching and power hitting. The starting staff featured Dave Stewart, who posted four straight 20-win seasons, starting in 1987, and Bob Welch, who in 1990 won 27 games and a Cy Young Award. The key to the A's pitching staff, however, was Dennis Eckersley, who may be the greatest relief pitcher of all time.

On offense, Oakland relied primarily on Mark and right fielder Jose Canseco, who teamed up to form one of the greatest home run-hitting duos in baseball history. Over the course of three seasons, Mark and Jose totaled 200 home runs and richly deserved their Bash Brothers nickname.

In 1988, his second full season, Mark hit 32 homers with 99 RBIs and was named the American League's starting first baseman in the All-Star Game. Those would have been great numbers for any other hitter in baseball, but when Mark hit "only" 32, people began to wonder what was wrong with him.

It wasn't that Mark wasn't as good a hitter as he was as a rookie, it was that the pitchers had gotten smarter about how they pitched to him. When Mark was a rookie, the pitchers didn't really know much about him. They didn't know the pitches he hit best. They didn't know which pitches were the most effective against him.

In the next few years, the pitchers did everything in their power to keep him from hitting the ball out of the park. They didn't give him very good pitches to hit and walked him a lot. Even Mark's mother got frustrated watching the way opposing hurlers kept the ball away from him. "He's lucky if he sees one good pitch a game," she complained. "It's almost like it's not fair."

Mark was also hampered in the later part of the season by a herniated disc in his lower back, a condition that has continued to plague him throughout his career. But the A's were so talented that they could absorb the dip in Mark's power numbers and still post an almost gaudy 104–58 record, romping to the American League's Western Division title by 13 games over the second-place Minnesota Twins.

The A's continued merrily along, sweeping four straight against the Boston Red Sox in the American League Championship Series. Their joyride was derailed, however, by the Los Angeles Dodgers, a Cinderella team that had shocked the Mets in the National League Championship Series.

The mighty A's were big favorites to beat the Dodgers in the World Series. But, thanks to the pitching of Cy Young Award winner Orel Hershiser, who beat the A's twice, and a dramatic ninth-inning, pinch-hit game-winning home run in the Series opener by the injured Kirk Gibson, the Dodgers beat the odds and the A's, in five games.

In terms of disappointment, the Series ranked right up there with the Olympic loss for Mark. Not only did his team lose the world championship, but he managed to collect only one hit in 17 at-bats.

Ironically, though, Mark's one hit was the biggest hit of his career, a bottom of the ninth, two out, game-winning home run that gave the A's their only win in the series.

"I was more or less numb, running around the bases," Mark said. "Kids always dream of hitting one like that. You play in the street, and it's always the bottom of the ninth in the World Series. That was my favorite home run of them all."

Mark's back problems worsened in 1989. He missed 15 days in April and played the rest of the season in pain. He still managed to put up some impressive power numbers, knocking in 95 runs and hitting 33 homers, the third highest total in the AL behind Canseco and Fred McGriff, who had stroked 34 for the Toronto Blue Jays. His batting average, though, dipped to .231, a career low.

Once again, the A's dominated the American League. They finished the season with a 99–63 record, seven games ahead of the Kansas City Royals in the AL West, and needed just five games to beat the Blue Jays and advance to their second straight World Series. This time, the opponent was the San Francisco Giants, Oakland's next-door neighbors.

The series opened in Oakland, where the A's made it look easy by taking the two games by a combined 10–1 score. After one day off, the teams went across the bay to San Francisco's Candlestick Park for Game 3. But, just as the fans were settling into their seats, a powerful earthquake struck.

The stadium shook. The electricity went out.

Because earthquakes are fairly common in California, everyone knew what was happening. What they didn't know was how serious the earthquake was. It turned out that there was mass destruction in San Francisco and Oakland. The Bay Bridge was destroyed. Fires burned throughout the city, and 67 people were killed.

The Commissioner of Baseball, Fay Vincent, thought seriously about canceling the World Series. Some people believed that it would be disrespectful to the families of the people who died to continue playing the Series, especially in San Francisco. Vincent decided, though, that it would be good for the morale of the people in the Bay Area if the Series continued. So, ten days after the earthquake, the teams resumed play, and the A's picked up right where they left off, beating the Giants easily in both games, and sweeping the Series 4–0.

Although Mark ended up hitting .294 in the World Series, he was remarkably the only player in the A's starting lineup *not* to hit a home run. But he'll always trade home runs for a championship season.

In 1990, Mark again put up good, but not great, numbers. He hit 39 homers and knocked in 108 runs. In the process, he entered his name yet again in baseball's record books, becoming the first player in history to hit at least 30 homers in each of his first four seasons in the majors.

Despite his big offensive stats, Mark was most proud of his work on defense. During the year, he was involved in an amazing 1,429 plays and made only five errors. His .997 fielding percentage was good enough to earn him the Gold Glove award as the American League's best-fielding first baseman.

The A's, meanwhile, had turned in another spectacular regular seaon, winning 103 games before going on to sweep the Red Sox in the ALCS for the second time in three seasons. Oakland was a heavy favorite to repeat as World Series champs, but the Cincinnati Reds stunned the A's with a four-game sweep. The Reds acutally *crushed* the A's, winning 7–0, 1–0, 8–3, and 2–1. It was stunning that the A's, who were one of the best hitting teams in baseball, were held to only four runs in four games. And Mark wasn't much help, managing only three small singles in 14 World Series at-bats.

Years later, Mark admitted that he didn't fully appreciate the trio of championship seasons while they were happening. "I don't think any of us realized what we were doing at the time," he said. "We realized we were a good team. But I don't think we really knew how good we were.

"It was when we won the AL West, for the third year in a row, in Kansas City, nobody even ran out onto the field. Guys *walked* out onto the field. Right there, I realized a lot of guys were taking things for granted. I sort of regret that because now I want to get back there."

5. Down in the Dumps

Almost everyone has a time in life he or she would rather forget. For Mark, that time was the years that stretched from 1991 through 1994. In those four years, most everything that could go wrong did go wrong. It was a period that began with a horrible batting slump and ended with a series of injuries and operations.

At one point, things got so bad that Mark was on the verge of quitting the game.

From Day 1 of the 1991 season, it was clear that something was wrong. Suddenly, Mark couldn't hit. Not only couldn't he hit for power, he could hardly get his bat on the ball. His home run total dipped to 22, less than half the number he hit as a rookie, and his batting average plummeted to .201. LaRussa benched Mark for the final game of the year, sparing him from the embarrassing possibility of dropping below .200.

During the season, everyone was trying to give Mark advice on how to hit. "I must have gotten 100 suggestions and I listened to 90 of them," he said. "I can't count how many stances I had. I tried everything, and nothing worked. I tried a bunch of different bats. I even starting listening to the fans. But nothing really worked."

Mark, who had always been a happy-go-lucky guy in the A's clubhouse, was suddenly sullen and depressed. "For the first time in my life, I disliked baseball," he said. "It was frustrating answering the same question over and over, "Are you going to be able to hit .200?' It was frustrating trying to dig out of a hole that kept getting deeper and deeper."

Mark's problems on the field were compounded by problems at home. His marriage to Kathy had ended in divorce. His son, Matt, whom he loves dearly, was living with his mother 40 minutes away, and Mark found it lonely to go home every night to an empty house.

Some fair-weather fans also added to Mark's woes by turning against him, even though he had been such a tremendous hitter during his first four full seasons. He couldn't even escape the boos when he went home. One day, while sitting and trying to relax at his pool, he was distracted by the sound of voices coming from the Alamo Elementary School. The kids stood at the fence, looked down on Mark, and shouted "McGwire stinks."

Mark's slump coincided with an off-year for the A's. They finished the 1991 season with a record of 84–78, sinking to fourth place in the American League West. "That was definitely the lowest point in my career," noted Mark. "One day, during the off season, I drove all the way [from Oakland] down to Los Angeles. It's like five and a half hours, and I didn't turn on the radio. I thought about everything I needed to do in life. I started trying to get my mind back together. I started getting my life back together."

It was at that point that Mark decided to rededicate himself to being the best baseball player that he could be. The first thing he did was to start on an intense weight lifting regimen. Although he was big and strong to begin with, the weight training made him 25 pounds bigger and a whole lot stronger.

"The weight lifting relieved a lot of the pain I was going through after the 1991 season," Mark said. "When I started to see changes in my body, it made me feel a lot more positive, more confident in myself."

He also began doing eye exercises. Even though his contact lenses gave him 20–15 vision, he felt like he wasn't seeing the ball as clearly as he would have liked to when he was at bat. The eye exercises helped him focus clearly on the ball, from the time it left the pitcher's hand until it reached home plate. If a hitter can reduce his reaction time, even by a fraction of a second, it can add a whole lot of points to his batting average and increase his power totals.

"I had been through like a 100 different contact lenses, trying to find the ones that would help my astigmatism," he said. "But it turned out that I just needed to strengthen my eyes. There are muscles near the eye that most people just never develop."

Having taken care of his physical health, Mark also went about improving his self-esteem, which had plummeted along with his batting average. He began to see a psychiatrist, who helped Mark regain his confidence, and with it, his zest for life and his love for the game of baseball.

By the time spring training opened in 1992, it was obvious that Mark had performed a complete about-face. His teammates could see a change in his attitude, as could his manager. Mark walked into LaRussa's office and told him not to worry. He was back. "From that moment, I knew Mark was going to have a great season," LaRussa said. "You could just see that he had a whole new attitude. Maybe it was just his old attitude. Whatever it was, it was great to have him back."

During spring training, Mark worked closely with the A's new hitting coach, Doug Rader. Rader had watched Mark closely during the 1991 season, and what he saw he didn't like. He also saw that Mark was frustrated because he wasn't getting great pitches to hit. He saw that Mark was trying to hit every ball over the fence.

The first thing Rader did was shorten Mark's swing. He told Mark that he didn't have to swing with all his might to knock the ball over the wall. With his strength, all it took was a solid hit to send the ball flying.

Rader then worked with Mark on his pitch selection. Because pitchers weren't going to give him great pitches, Mark had to be patient. No more chasing balls out of the strike zone, no more trying to pull the ball when the pitch was on the outside part of the plate. "I had to realize that pitchers weren't going to be giving me great pitches to hit," Mark said. "I had to figure out what they were going to give me, then figure out what best to do with those pitches."

All the work paid off. Alhough Mark played in only 139 games, he hit 42 homers with 104 RBIs, and his batting averaged jumped 67 points, up to .268. The same kids who jeered him in 1991 were cheering him and begging him for his autograph in 1992. Even Mark's rookie card, which had dropped in value from $20 to $5 in 1991, was back up to $15.

That year, Mark finished fourth in the Most Valuable Player Award voting and cracked his 200th career home run. He reached the milestone in only 2,852 at bats, faster than all but four players in baseball history.

With Mark back in form, the A's also bounced back, finishing the year with a record of 96–66 and winning the AL West for the fourth time in five seasons. There would be no trip to the World Series this time, though, as Toronto beat Oakland in six games. Mark again struggled in the postseason, managing only three hits in 20 at bats.

Just when it appeared that things were looking up for Mark, his body betrayed him. Between 1993 and 1995, Mark missed 242 of 420 games. It all came down to physiology and physics.

Physiologically, his feet just don't match his body. At 6-5, with a muscular 240-pound frame, Mark is a massive physical specimen. His feet, though, are long and narrow, with small arches. When Mark runs hard, then stops quickly, as so often happens in baseball, it puts an enormous amount of pressure on his feet. In Mark's case, the pressure was so great that something had to give. That something was the heel on one of his feet. "I was a ticking time bomb," he said. "It was bad structure even at birth."

6. The Comeback Kid

After playing a combined 74 games in 1993 and 1994, Mark was beginning to wonder whether he'd ever play a full season again. But instead of sitting around and feeling sorry for himself, he spent a lot of his off-season time lifting weights, doing eye exercises, and working on his hitting.

To relax, Mark played some golf.

Despite his hard work, Mark began the 1995 season mired in a slump in which he was able to stroke only four hits in his first 18 at-bats. But before he could even think about a repeat of 1991, Mark broke out of the slump and began an 18-game hitting streak, the longest such streak of his career.

Then, in June, Mark started cranking out home runs at an amazing rate. He hit two homers against the Red Sox on June 10, then added three more on June 11. The homers continued at a steady pace throughout the month. He finished June off with a game-winning grand slammer in the bottom of the ninth against Lee Smith, one of the toughest relief pitchers in the league.

The good times quickly turned into the scariest moment of his career, however, when David Cone, one of the hardest throwers in the league, hit Mark in the helmet with a fastball.

The crowd went silent as Mark fell to the ground. They were terrified that Cone had broken Mark's skull. Fortunately for Mark, it was "only" a concussion.

The timing couldn't have been much worse, though, because Mark was slated to be the starting first baseman in the All-Star Game. It had been three years since Mark had played in an All-Star Game, and he was extremely disappointed when his doctors told him that he was in no condition to fly.

When the All-Star break ended, Mark's hard luck continued.

In July, he spent more time on the bench than on the field, missing 12 games with a bruised foot and then another 21 contests with a sore back.

When he came back, however, he did so with a vengeance, hitting the ball as well as he ever had in his career. Mark swatted 11 homers in his final 18 games, to finish the season with 39 homers in only 104 games and only 317 at bats. His home run rate, one homer for every 8.1 at bats, was a major league record, breaking the standard of one homer for every 8.5 at bats set by Babe Ruth back in 1920. If Mark had been able to play in a full 162-game season, he might have approached, or even eclipsed, Roger Maris's record of 61 home runs in a season.

Mark had become a more disciplined hitter, a fact that could be evidenced by his 88 base-on-balls and his .274 batting average, his best showing since his rookie season.

"I really began to use my head," explained Mark. "I'd take the time to think about what each pitcher did in different situations. So much of the game is mental, and it took me a long time to figure that out. Your physical tools last just so long. It's what you do with your mental tools that keeps you in the game."

After his increased understanding of hitting had helped him produce his best season in eight years, Mark began looking forward to the opening of 1996's spring training camp. In March, though, disaster struck again when he blew out his right heel during an exhibition game and was put on the disabled list for the eighth time in his career. The original prognosis was that he was going to be out for three months.

Mark couldn't believe this was happening again. Not only did he face the prospect of missing half of yet another season, he was also looking at months of painful rehabilitation. Having gone through this so often in the past few years, Mark wasn't sure whether he was up to the task of doing it again.

Alhough he was only 32 years old, Mark began to seriously consider retirement. "I was pretty close to it," he admitted. "I didn't think I could go through another rehab. I had done it twice, getting back to a competitive level, and then it happened for a third time—with no assurance that I wouldn't have to do it again, even sooner."

When Mark shared his feelings with his family, they advised him to go through the rehab process and return to the A's. "Everybody left me with the feeling that I couldn't walk away from something I had done my whole life," he said. "If I did, they told me, I would regret it for the rest of my life."

Ultimately, though, it was Mark's father who convinced him to go back and give it one more try. John knew all about battling back from adversity. When his polio was diagnosed, he was told that he might never walk again. He spent seven months in bed before he could even begin the long, difficult process of learning to simply take steps again. "He told me that if I retired, it would be the biggest mistake of my life."

With his dad as his role model, Mark showed that he had the mental toughness to overcome the hard-luck hand that he had drawn by working day and night to get his heel better. During his rehabilitation, he also had a chance to think about his life, about baseball. "I sat back and watched the game and really admired what I had," he said. "I think that everybody, some time during their career, might take for granted what they have.

"Maybe the injury was a little blessing. I look back and see the great teams I've been on and the great players I've played with and I think I appreciate the game more than I ever have."

Although Mark's injury was supposed to keep him sidelined until June, his diligent rehab program allowed him to return to the starting lineup by April 26. After a short period of adjustment, Mark began to find his stroke and celebrated May Day by crushing a grand slam off Phil Leftwich and the California Angels. On May 20, Mark smashed his sixth homer of the season against the Boston Red Sox, the same day that Mo Vaughn, Boston's first baseman and the league's reigning MVP, poked his 17th round tripper.

The idea that Mark, who finished the month with 11 dingers, might even become a contender for the 1996 home run title seemed so far fetched at that point that nobody even had it on their radar scope.

Mark, though, was in a serious groove and sporting a .327 batting average as the calendar flipped to June. He kept up his torrid pace throughout the month, compiling a .326 average while collecting 25 RBIs and 14 dingers in only 26 games. Number 14 for the month was the 25th of the season as well as the 300th of Mark's career.

In July, as the weather got hotter, so did Mark. He added 13 more homers and 21 RBIs, finishing the month with his 38th dinger, a 488-foot blast off Paul Quantrill at Toronto's SkyDome. The ball went into the fifth deck, the longest home run ever hit in the building and the longest hit in the majors in five years.

Mark's teammate, Scott Brosius, was furious with himself because he had chose, that moment to go into the clubhouse for a soda. "That was my biggest mistake of the season," Brosius said. "It's a mistake ever to miss one of his at-bats. Players aren't usually big fans, but he's a guy you can't help but be in awe of. I mean, this guy is the best home run hitter of them all, he's unbelievable."

Geronomo Berroa agreed. "You never know how far he's going to hit it," added Berroa, the A's outfielder/designated hitter, who poked 36 homers of his own in 1996. "I mean, there are times you just stand there and wonder whether it's ever going to land."

Mark is almost embarrassed by the attention his long homers have gotten. "When I broke in, they didn't keep track of things the way they do now." Mark, who added a 475-footer against the Minnesota Twins and a 470-footer against the White Sox said, "These days, they have a stat for how many times a guy goes for a cup of coffee."

Ironically, Mark picked August, the hottest month of the year, to cool down. It wasn't until August 12 that he recorded his 40th homer. For the month, he hit eight homers, a respectable, but not a record-threatening, number. As he entered September, Mark was well within reach of the 50–home run plateau, but his chances of reaching 60 were virtually nil.

No. 47 came on September 6 and was quickly followed by No. 48 on September 7. That's when the pressure of going for No. 50 started really kicking in. Mark didn't hit another until September 14, on a day on which the A's were playing a doubleheader against the Cleveland Indians.

In Game 1, he went up against Charles Nagy, who came into the game with a record of 15–4. In the bottom of the first, with two outs and Jose Herrera on first, Mark took the Cleveland ace downtown for his 49th homer of the year. Then, in the nightcap, Cleveland served up Chad Ogea, one of the top-rated young pitchers in the game. Like Nagy, Ogea decided to challenge Mark early, and Mac responded by swatting the ball over the fence for his 50th home run of the season.

All Mark could think about, as he rounded the bases, was that he had to get hold of the ball, because he had promised his son, Matt, that he would give him No. 50 and didn't want to break the promise. "Everything I do in life and baseball is for Matt," Mark explained. "It is just unbelievable. To accomplish it ten years later, and have my son be a part of it, that's very, very special. I don't know how much he understands about what I've done, but I think it means a lot to him."

Mark finished the season with 52 homers, nine short of Maris's record, but more than any other hitter in baseball.

"I never took it too seriously," he said of the race to beat Maris. "Pitchers have been working me so tough, I'm happy to get to 50. I might get one good pitch to drive a night, and I might foul it back.

"Only 12 guys had ever done it before I did," he said. "But

nobody seems to talk about the 50-homer mark. Twelve is not too many for the thousands who have played the game. So it's a nice class to be in."

The class got a little bigger on the final day of the 1996 season when Brady Anderson, the Baltimore Oriole's centerfielder, hit his 50th. It was the first time that two players had hit 50 or more homers in the same season since teammates Mickey Mantle and Roger Maris did it in 1961.

While Anderson was hitting his 50th on the last day of the season, Mark sat out the A's final game. He was simply drained, both physically and emotionally.

"I just want to be a normal person again," he said, looking forward to the off-season. "It will be nice to get out of the old rat race. It will be nice to just be Mark McGwire the person. Not Mark McGwire the athlete."

Mark finished the year leading the majors in homers, slugging percentage (.730), and on-base percentage (.467). Only nine other players in history have ever completed that trifecta. Mark, though, may have been proudest of his .312 batting average, a testament to his discipline at the plate.

"He was just unbelievable," Mark's manager, Art Howe, said. "When you think of what he went through, from the beginning of the season, to get to where he got there haven't been many seasons like that."

7. Hall of Famer?

After ten years in the Major Leagues, ten rollercoaster seasons filled with joys and disappointments, Mark is more focused than he's ever been.

He is looking forward to the 1997 season more than any other season before. Physically, he's as strong as he's ever been, and his health is as good as it's been in years. In addition, he's mentally tougher than he's ever been.

Once the type of player who loved to blend into the background, Mark has established himself as the A's team leader. "I definitely will speak out now," he said. "If something's on my mind, I'll say it. I was never like that before."

The A's are a team filled with young, talented players. For the first time since 1992, there is reason to believe they will make a run for the American League pennant in 1997.

"I've been enjoying the game of baseball more than ever," Mark said. "I enjoy being with these young guys. I'm not one of those guys who sits there and says, "Oh, I've got this ego. I can't talk to these guys. I can't go out with them.' I mean, I love hanging out with them. I love talking to them."

Mark knows that everyone will expect him to make another run at Roger Maris this year. He also knows he needs to stay healthy, needs to have a lot of luck, and needs to keep focused to do it.

Mark is certain that Maris's record will be broken. He has serious doubts, though, that he will be the one to break it. He points to players like Albert Belle and Ken Griffey, Jr. as two players with the ability to do the job.

"Some day, somebody is going to break the home run record," he said. "And it will be an unbelievable feat. But I won't sit here thinking about it because I realize how difficult it is.

"I mean, hitting a home run is probably the most difficult thing in sports, and doing it consistently in the second half of a season—when teams aren't pitching it to you—is mind boggling.

"Most power hitters don't see a lot to hit through a game, a week, a month. It's no fun, but that's what happens when you hit home runs. People don't want to pitch to you."

Although Mark loves the game more now than at any other time, he also knows he can step away with no regrets. His first priority in life is his son Matt, with whom he spends as much time as he can. "Matt is a constant reminder to me that there's more to life than baseball."

Mark isn't about to retire any time soon, though. He desperately wants to go to another World Series. He wants to collect a few more homers. He knows he hasn't put up Hall of Fame numbers yet, but a couple of more monster seasons like 1996 could clinch the deal.

Although some people note that Mark would have earned his ticket to Cooperstown by now if he hadn't missed so much time to injuries, Mark doesn't look on the past as a series of missed opportunities.

"I've never been a guy that said, 'What if?'" said Mark, who has averaged one homer for every 12.41 at-bats for his career, second only behind Babe Ruth's one homer for every 11.76 at-bats on the all time list. "You can't succeed as a player or as a human being if you do that. You're not moving forward. You'd always be doubting yourself and wondering.

"There's no sense living in the past or thinking about the what-ifs. I'm happy with who I am and where I am. I really feel like I'm just getting into my prime, with a lot of good baseball ahead of me."

PHOTO SECTION

Mark McGwire, a rare member of the 50-homer club.
Courtesy of the Oakland A's

Hoping for something good to hit.
Courtesy of the Oakland A's

Going, going…
Photo by Michael Zagaris

Gone!
Photo by Michael Zagaris

Gold Glove Form
Photo by Sportschrome East/West

Greetings from Atlanta
Courtesy of the Atlanta Baseball Team

Chipper from the left side
Courtesy of the Atlanta Baseball Team

Chipper from the right side
Photo by Michael Zagaris

Another base hit
Photo by Rob Tringali Jr. Sportschrome East/West

At the hot corner
Photo by Michael Zito Sportschrome East/West

CHIPPER JONES

1. Born to Play Baseball

Every kid who ever threw a strike or hit a homer or made a great catch knows the dream—the dream of being a professional baseball player.

It's the great American fantasy to be up at the plate in the bottom of the ninth inning of the seventh game of the World Series and smash the winning home run high over the outfield fence.

Some kids, though, do more than dream.

Those are the kids who seem to spend every waking moment playing or practicing. They're the ones who throw balls until their arms can't throw anymore. They're the ones hitting balls off a tee until their hands are sore and blistered. They're the ones who come inside only after it's way too dark to see.

Chipper Jones was one of *those* kids. He's also one of the few whose dream of actually becoming a professional ball player actually came true.

Today, as a member of the Atlanta Braves, Chipper is one of the hottest young players in the major leagues. He's already played in two World Series and one All-Star Game. And he's not even 25 years old.

Chipper Jones was born on April 24, 1972, in Deland, Florida, and grew up in a small town called Pierson, which is located about 40 miles west of Daytona Beach.

Until Chipper came along, things were pretty quiet in Pierson. For as long as people can remember, the sign leading into town read "Pierson—the Fern Capital of the World." These days, it also reads, "and hometown of Chipper Jones."

"Chipper" was named Larry Wayne Jones, Jr. at birth. But, from the time he was a toddler, his parents, Larry, Sr. and Lynne, called him Chipper, because Larry Jones, Jr. looked and acted exactly like his father. The similarities were so great, his parents started calling him "a chip off the old block." Eventually, it became just "Chipper." Today, hardly any one calls him *Larry.*

"Chipper is a good name," he said. "If I were called Larry Jones, who'd remember that? Chipper is one of those first names people remember. Think of Cal (Ripken, Jr.), and Mickey (Mantle). You hear those names and you say, 'Those were some of the best to ever play the game.' I'd like to be thought of like that someday."

In Chipper, Larry, Sr. saw a reflection of all of the dreams of his youth. He, too, had been one of those kids who dreamed about becoming a professional baseball player. Only his dreams didn't quite come true.

In his day, Larry Jones was a good enough high school shortstop to be selected by the Chicago Cubs late in the 1967 Amateur Draft, but not so good that he didn't have to wait until hundreds of other players had already been taken.

Larry knew that the odds were heavily stacked against him ever making it all the way to Wrigley Field. So, he was willing to be convinced by his dad to accept a baseball scholarship from Stetson University in Deland, Florida. It was, by one measure, a simple question of economics and expectations. A college education was going to be worth a lot more money and security than the Cubs were offering to a late-round draft pick.

Larry and his dad knew that major league teams draft nearly 2,000 players each year in an attempt to stock all their minor league teams. Many of the players who are selected weigh their odds and their options and never even sign a contract. The vast majority of those players who do sign a contract never make it past the low-level minors and then have to find a way to craft a life's work for themselves.

Larry went on to earn baseball All-America honors at Stetson. He also came home with a college degree in education and coaching, tools that have served him throughout his professional life. But, he never forgot the dream that he had set aside; the dream that he wanted to pass on to his only child, Chipper.

The process of turning Chipper into a major leaguer began even before he could even walk, when his mother would put him in his stroller and walk him over to the field where Larry was coaching the Taylor High School varsity baseball team. By the time Chipper could crawl, he was all over the field. He would chase after loose baseballs and pretend to swing a bat.

When Chipper was three years old, the formal training began. Larry would patiently toss the whiffle ball, underhanded, to Chipper. Even then, Chipper demonstrated remarkable hand-eye coordination. From the whiffle ball and the plastic bat, Chipper graduated to a T-ball bat and a tennis ball.

When he was a little older, during the baseball season, Chipper and his father would watch the Baseball Game of the Week every Saturday. As they watched, Larry began introducing his son to the subtleties of the game. He'd point out what kind of pitches the pitcher was throwing, where the fielders were standing, and what sort of batting stance each hitter used.

They would carefully go over the roster of each team, and Chipper would quickly learn the strengths and weaknesses of every player. With pitchers, he'd learn what their favorite pitches were. He'd even learn which kind of pitches they'd throw in pressure situations.

When the game was over, father and son would go outside to replay the game in the yard. "If the guy due up was a lefthander, I'd hit lefthanded," Chipper recalled. "Then, when a righty came up, I'd switch around. It was more fun that way. We stood out there and just hit. That's why I'm such a good fastball hitter today."

Larry never gave Chipper any breaks. Even when Chipper was just six or seven years old, Larry would throw the ball fast. In the early years, Chipper could hardly get his bat on the ball. Rather than quit, though, Chipper just worked harder. As the years went on, not only was Chipper starting to get hits, he was starting to beat his father. By the time Chipper was 13, the tables had been turned. After one game in which Chipper crushed his father, Larry went inside to his wife and said, "I can't beat him anymore, Lynne, this is scary."

Then their game moved from the confines of the backyard to the batting cages at Taylor High School. Chipper would actually spot his father four runs, then almost always come back to win. Any grounder or pop fly was an out. It took a line drive to get on base or advance hitters.

"This is a family that will compete over the time of day," Larry said. "It wasn't like we were playing for a lot of money or anything. We'd compete for a soda. Chipper will compete with you in dominoes, Scrabble, gin rummy—just like he's playing the seventh game of the World Series. His work ethic and his competitiveness probably do more for him than his ability."

While Larry worked with Chipper on the technical aspects of baseball, Lynne tutored him in the mental aspects of sports. Lynne, who had been a champion equestrian rider, helped imbue her son with a sense of supreme confidence.

"My mom instilled in me early that you need a necessary arrogance to be able to compete," Chipper said. "Especially in this game. Whenever I need a pep talk, she's always there to kick me in the butt and get me back on track with the mental part. Most guys, when their mom suggests something, roll their eyes. When *my* mom does, I listen. My mom knows more about baseball than half the people in the major leagues.

"Together, my parents taught me the fine line between arrogance and what we call quiet confidence. You don't go around showing anybody up, but you can still have that swagger, that walk that let's the other guy know you are going to beat him."

Lynne was usually close by when Chipper was practicing or playing. Often, she would videotape his games. When they got back home, the whole family would watch the tapes, with both parents offering constructive criticism. They would go over every at-bat, every play in the field, just to see ways in which Chipper could improve his game.

When Chipper wasn't watching videotapes of himself, he was watching great players from the past. His father had a collection of videos of great players and great games in baseball history. Larry's favorite player was Mickey Mantle, a tough, fast, hard-hitting switch-hitter for the Yankees.

"I guess you could say that I grew up in Mickey Mantle's shadow," Chipper said. "My father was a huge Mickey Mantle fan. That's why I'm a switch-hitter. My dad wanted me to be able to play like him."

Of course, there were times when Chipper didn't want to practice or play. He'd rather play with his friends or just watch televison. "My dad always told me that when I wasn't working, there was always someone else out there working," Chipper said. "That was something I always took to heart."

"My dad taught me that a whole lot of guys have talent. The ones who make it are the ones who work. On my team, I want the guy who has the work ethic and desire. I don't want the guy with a lot of talent and a bad attitude."

When Chipper began playing Little League, it almost wasn't fair. Most of the other kids were playing for the first time in their lives. Chipper, at the age of eight, had a better understanding of the fundamentals and techniques of baseball than most high school players did.

In the three seasons that Chipper played Little League, his teams went 78–3, and Chipper was the best hitter, the best pitcher, and the best shortstop in the entire league. His manager, Richard Hagstrom, had never seen anything like him. "We all knew just as well as we knew our names that this kid was destined to go someplace," Hagstrom said.

When Chipper was 12, he hit three home runs against an

Altamonte Springs, Florida, team that went on to play in the Little League World Series. "It was kind of scary, but I said to Lynne that day that I think Chipper may be one of the ten best players in his age group in the country," Larry recalled.

Two years later, as a 14-year-old eighth grader, it was clear that Chipper had the ability to play for the Taylor High School varsity baseball team. The only problem was that his dad was the coach. Larry didn't want anyone to think that it was favoritism that got Chipper his spot on the team, so Larry resigned as the baseball coach. The new coach was so impressed with Chipper's ability that he not only put him on the varsity squad, he named Chipper as his starting second baseman, sending a senior to the bench.

In ninth grade, Chipper established himself as one of the stars of the varsity team, but he let his success go to his head. Although he was only 15, Chipper was being treated like a hero. He wasn't working hard in his classes, but he was given A's and B's. And, although his sheer talent allowed him to be a standout on the diamond, he wasn't practicing as hard as he could have. "They started doing itty-bitty favors for him," Larry said. "They were cutting him slack in class. That wasn't fair to him or to the other kids."

This is not the way Larry wanted Chipper to grow up. Bad habits learned in high school, Larry knew, could last a lifetime.

He took Chipper on the two-hour drive to Jacksonville to look at The Bolles School, a private school in that had an excellent reputation, both academically and athletically. Larry believed that Chipper needed a kick in the pants, and Bolles was a good place for him to get it.

"We took Chipper to see the school and to make his own decision," Larry said. "He's the one who made the big decision." But, it was a decision Chipper quickly regretted, at least in the short term.

It was the first time in his life he had really been away from his family and from Day One, he was horribly homesick.

In his first year at Bolles, Chipper called his parents almost every day. Tearfully, he would complain about the difficulty of the work and the snobbishness of the other kids. "There were lots of nights I'd cry and say, 'Get me out of this place,' Chipper said. "I wasn't making good grades. Homework was piling up. I didn't know how to budget my time."

"I told him that coming home was not an option," Larry said. "Kids give what we demand of them, not what we ask of them. He made a 3.2 grade point average (B+) that first year, and he maintained it."

Chipper did have problems, however, fitting in with the other students at Bolles. Having come from a middle-class background, he found he was a bit intimidated by his wealthier classmates. "The school was totally rich, snobby, private," he said. "I'd come to school in my little 1983 Ford Escort and park next to a row of BMWs and Preludes and Porsches—all these cars *my classmates* were driving."

Jones fit right in on the baseball field, however. In 27 games, he hit .375, with seven homers and 26 runs batted in. Surprisingly, though, Chipper slumped the following year, but Bolles had such a strong team that they were able to win the Florida State Championship despite Chipper's .270 batting average.

In his senior year at Bolles, Chipper got back on track and emerged as one of the top prep school players in the country. He not only got it done in the field and at bat, where he compiled an astounding .483 average with five homers and 27 RBI, but he also turned in a 7–3 record as a pitcher with a microscopic earned run average of 0.98.

"He was born to play baseball," said his Bolles coach, Don Suriano. "I think God reached out and touched him. As a sophomore, I viewed him as a senior. As a senior, he was playing like a junior in college. Chipper was just a guy who could carry a team on his back. I'll never have another kid like him."

Chipper was able to accomplish all this despite the fact that he knew that major league scouts and college coaches were watching every move he made. "There must have been 20, 25 scouts in the stands for every game my senior year," Chipper said. "At first, it was a lot of pressure, but I got used to it."

The only sour note in an otherwise brilliant season occurred the day before Bolles was scheduled to play in its second consecutive State Championship game. Chipper's teammates, it seems, had been taunting another player on the team, and Chipper walked up to see what was happening.

"The other guys on the club started picking on him, and he got mad at everybody," Chipper said. "I just walked into it. He started yelling at me. I told him to get out of my face. He began pushing me, and I hit him."

The other kid ended up with six stitches in his face. Chipper ended up with a broken bone in his right hand, his pitching hand.

"We went back to the hotel, and his hand was all swollen. I asked Chipper whether he thought he could pitch in the Championship Game," Suriano said. "He just looked up at me and said, 'I'll go.'"

Not only did Chipper "go," he pitched a great game. The broken bone kept him from throwing his curve ball, so he had to rely strictly on his fastball. Despite that handicap, Chipper pitched Bolles to within one out of a 2–1 victory that never happened, because an error led to the tying run and an eventual 3–2 defeat.

Chipper, was not only disappointed by the loss, he was also concerned about what other people, including major league scouts, would think about his fight the previous day. "I've got to take responsibility for my own actions," he said. "I just don't want people to think that I'm a big bully. It was both our faults. It happened, it was over quickly and we both apologized. I just want the major league teams to know that I'm not some head case."

Ironically, the fight actually would up enhancing Chipper's

status in the eyes of scouts, some of whom tend to question the toughness of players who come from private schools, and usually privileged backgrounds. "God works in strange ways, sometimes," shrugged Suriano. "Chipper took a bad incident and made it work in his favor. If the Braves or anyone else wondered about his intestinal fortitude, they found out quickly how tough he was and how much he wants to play."

Chipper had more than just baseball scouts watching him. He was also an excellent basketball and football player. As a senior wide receiver, Chipper earned All-State honors in football. Three of the biggest football powers in the country, the University of Southern California, the University of California at Los Angeles, and Stanford University, all offered him football scholarships.

The University of Miami didn't offer Chipper a football scholarship, but they did offer him a baseball scholarship. Not knowing whether any professional team was going to sign him, Chipper signed a letter of intent to go to Miami beginning in the fall of 1990. "I'll just have to see how it goes in the draft," Chipper said. "If I don't end up signing (with the pros), I'll go to Miami. I don't think I can lose, either way."

2. I'm No. 1!

As the days of the 1990 June Amateur Draft drew closer, Chipper, still wearing a cast on his hand, became more and more edgy, wondering which team would draft him. He hoped that the Atlanta Braves, the team that had the number one overall pick, would use it on him.

Chipper liked the fact that Atlanta was the major league city closest to his family's home in Pierson. He also realized that he might have a fast track to the big time if he signed with Atlanta, a franchise that seemed to have a permanent lock on last place in the National League's Western Division (Atlanta was switched to the NL East before the start of the 1994 season).

Atlanta, likewise, had a great deal of interest in Chipper. Bobby Cox, the team's general manager at the time (and later Chipper's first manager in the major leagues), had personally scouted Chipper on four separate occasions. But, the top spot on Atlanta's wish list was a righthanded high school pitching sensation from Texas named Todd Van Poppel.

The scouts all said that Van Poppel was the best pitching prospect since another Texas schoolboy, Nolan Ryan, turned pro in 1965 and then set the big league career records for strikeouts (5,714) and no-hitters (seven).

Cox traveled to Texas before the draft and offered the pitching prodigy a three-year, $1 million contract. But Van Poppel said he wasn't interested in signing with a sad-sack franchise like Atlanta, or any other organization, other than the Oakland A's, who were the reigning World Series champions. Van Poppel even issued a statement saying that if he were drafted by any team other than the A's, he would accept a scholarship from the University of Texas rather than turn pro.

Cox was disappointed, but not crushed, by Van Poppel's rejection, because he knew that he had Chipper waiting in the wings. And, according to Cox, Chipper was the first "can't miss" prospect since Ken Griffey, Jr. had signed with the Seattle Mariners in 1987.

"Griffey is absolutely a natural," Cox said. "He can do it all. Chipper is the same way. He was born to play baseball. If you had watched him in Little League you'd have said, 'That kid's going to be a major league player.' We're delighted to get a shortstop of his ability. He already has excellent defensive ability, along with tremendous speed and the ability to switch, hit. We feel he's a high-quality talent at a position that's difficult to fill."

Unlike some players, who hold out for weeks, even months before signing their first contract, Chipper was so anxious to get his professional career started that he signed a contract the same day as the draft was held.

Paul Snyder, a team vice president who was at the Jones home, presented an offer that the Jone's countered with one of their own. After Snyder said the counteroffer was too high, Chipper and his father went upstairs for a private meeting.

"Chipper, you know we can get more money than this," said Larry.

Chipper, who never had more than a few extra dollars in his pocket at any one time, couldn't even conceive of the kind of numbers that were being thrown around. All he could think about was playing baseball, about taking the first step on his trip to the major leagues.

"I don't care about the money, Dad," Chipper said. "I want to be playing professional baseball in two weeks."

So, Larry came downstairs and offered to split the difference. Snyder agreed, and Chipper signed a deal that gave him a package worth $400,000, including a $275,000 signing bonus.

Shortly after signing that contract, Chipper quietly did a

favor for his old high school coach. He took part of his signing bonus and gave it to The Bolles School to fund the construction of an office for Coach Suriano.

"It was kind of a payback to my coach and my school and baseball program for helping me out," he said. "We had a great field and cages and stuff. But we didn't have much of a locker room. My coach didn't even have an office."

Van Poppel also reached his short-term goal when he signed a $1.2 million contract with the A's. But, he has never come close to living up to his star billing and the high expectations that were held for him. Traded by the A's to the Detroit Tigers in the middle of the 1996 season, Van Poppel has never even had a winning season. Through 1996, his record is 20–31.

3. Minor League Marvel

Two weeks after signing his contract, Chipper had his wish and was playing for Bradenton (Florida), Atlanta's entry in the Gulf Coast League. But the dream quickly turned into a nightmarish experience when Chipper, whose right hand still hadn't healed, wasn't able to throw well and couldn't crack the .230 mark in his 44 games with Bradenton.

Bradenton manager Glenn Hubbard, who had been Atlanta's starting second baseman from 1979 through 1987, didn't know about Chipper's still-mending hand and was wondering whether the team had made a big mistake in taking Chipper. "To be honest, when he first signed, I didn't know whether this was a smart draft pick," Hubbard said. "He was overmatched at the plate in rookie ball. I had no idea about his hand."

Although Hubbard worried about Chipper's abilities, he never questioned the kid's work ethic. Chipper took more batting practice than anyone and stayed for more fielding practice. "One thing sticks out in my mind," Hubbard said. "We had one week left in our season and we had an off day. There was optional batting practice, and who was the only guy who showed up? Chipper Jones."

Chipper recalls that summer as one of the worst experiences of his life. Some newspapers were already calling him a "flop." "It was embarrassing, just terrible," he said. "Being hurt, not being able to play as well as I wanted to, it really put me down in the dumps. I was beginning to wonder whether I'd ever live up to the expectations of other people."

After the season, Chipper went home to his family and spent a lot of time working out with his father, just as they had done for so many years before. "Chipper and his father are absolute clones," smiled Chipper's mother. "They stand the same way.

They walk the same. They even field the same. Watching Chipper play shortstop in high school was like watching Larry play shortstop in college.

"When Chipper came home and wanted his father to throw him a little batting practice, then next thing you know, Larry's trying to strike him out and Chipper's trying to hit home runs. But, that's what makes them so good at what they do."

After those winter workouts with his dad, Chipper dispelled everyone's doubts, including his own, when he hit .326, swatted 15 dingers, drove in 98 runs, and scored 104 for Atlanta's Class A farm team in Macon, Georgia. "I really needed a year like that one," said Chipper, who was named the South Atlantic League's Player of the Year. "I needed it to help myself mentally, and I needed it to put me back up there with the top prospects. It was very satisfying."

There was something else very satisfying about that year. While playing in Macon, Chipper met Karin Fulford and decided, almost immediately, that this was the woman he was going to marry.

"I don't know about this," said Larry. He worried that his son, who was only 19 years old, was too young to get married. But Chipper put an end to the discussion when he said, "Dad, she's just like Mom."

The couple married the following March, right before the start of the baseball season. "Getting married this [young] might not be for everyone," Chipper acknowledged. "But I believe I have met someone who makes me very happy and who will give stability to my life."

Chipper had assumed, based on his play at Macon, that he would start the 1992 season at the Double-A level. But, Chipper's play in spring training was so disappointing that he was promoted only to the Durham Bulls, Atlanta's top Single-A club. Although Chipper didn't post monster numbers with the Bulls, the franchise must have liked what they saw, because he was promoted to Atlanta's Double-A team in Greenville, South Carolina.

In Greenville, Chipper's bat came to life once again. In 67 games, he hit .346, including one torrid stretch in which he hit safely in 27 of 28 games. Phil Roof, who played in the major leagues for 15 years, had the misfortune of managing against Chipper in Double-A ball. Roof, who managed the Orlando Sting Rays, was dazzled as much by Chipper's play on defense as he was by the young phenom's work with the stick. "I've never seen a better minor league shortstop, anytime, anywhere," Roof said. "I guarantee you, that youngster is going to be an impact player in the major leagues."

When Greenville came to Jacksonville to play the Jacksonville Suns, the stadium was packed with Chipper's friends, his ex-teammates, and, of course, his family. The mayor of Jacksonville declared it to be "Chipper Jones Day," and Chipper was presented with the key to the city. "Chipper's mom and I are very proud of what he's doing," Larry said. "We'd love to see him playing in Atlanta, but we know he just isn't ready yet."

Chipper, however, continued his march to the big leagues the following season by tatooing Triple-A pitching for a .325 average while starring for Richmond (Virginia), the franchise's affiliate in the International League. And then, on September 10, 1993, Chipper received the call he had been waiting for ever since he had started playing backyard practice games with his father.

Because Atlanta was involved in a down-to-the-wire divisional race against the San Francisco Giants, Chipper mostly sat and watched, collecting two hits in only three at-bats. Although he was thrilled to be realizing his childhood dream of being on a major league team, he was disappointed that he wasn't given the opportunity to contribute to the team's successful run to the divisional title.

For his play at Richmond, Chipper was named Atlanta's

AAA minor league Player of the Year, and *Baseball America* called Chipper the No. 2 prospect in the entire International League.

4. The Lost Season

During the winter, it became almost a foregone conclusion that Chipper would replace Atlanta shortstop Jeff Blauser on his way to winning the 1994 Rookie of the Year Award. But, a season-ending injury to Ron Gant, Atlanta's slugging leftfielder, scrambled the plans of manager Bobby Cox. Cox, who was wary of replacing two veterans at the same time, decided that Chipper, instead of starting at shortstop, would have to compete for the opening in left field with two other highly touted rookies, Ryan Klesko and Tony Tarasco.

Chipper responded to the challenge with an unbelievable spring training show that included a .361 average, with two doubles, two homers, and eight RBIs in 36 at-bats. That virtuoso performance caused Cox to pencil Chipper in as his opening day left fielder and his No. 3 hitter. On March 18, though, disaster struck during an exhibition game against the New York Yankees.

The game, ironically, began on a trio of high notes. Chipper blasted a homer off Yankees starter Terry Mulholland and then made a pair of spectacular running catches in the outfield.

Later in the game, though, as Chipper tried to beat out an infield hit by avoiding a tag at first base, he twisted his body away from the glove and heard a horrible pop in his knee. The sound he heard was the tearing of the anterior cruciate ligament, the material that holds the thigh bone to the lower leg bone. When the anterior cruciate ligament tears, the knee has no support. It took nearly two weeks merely for the swelling in the knee to subside to the point where a team of physicians could perform reconstructive surgery on the knee.

Chipper was devastated when he was told that it would take 10 to 12 months for the knee to heal. But, he refused to accept the total loss of the 1994 season and, instead, optimistically set

August 31—the deadline for teams to file their postseason roster—as his targeted return date. If he could make the roster, and Atlanta made it into the playoffs, Chipper wanted to have the opportunity to participate and contribute.

When Chipper was first injured, he was so disappointed that he didn't even want to watch Atlanta's games on television. It was too frustrating for him to watch other guys on the field, especially Klesko and Tarasco. "After a while, I was able to watch again," Chipper said. "Then I really became a fan. Just watching them, I realized that these guys can flat-out play. I realized that this was a team I wanted to be a part of."

Chipper used the same discipline in coming back from his injury that he had always applied to his baseball. He spent hours each day lifting weights, stretching, walking, riding his stationary bike, working with a Stairmaster. . . anything to speed his recovery. Just ten weeks after his surgery, Chipper was walking without a limp. He worked out like a madman. But just when it looked like he might be back in time to play, yet another catastrophe hit. The major league baseball players went on strike. It was a strike that would kill the remainder of the 1994 season.

"Chipper's heart beats for baseball," Karin said. "In 1994, he lost baseball in two ways. He had an injury that made him realize that you never know when the game is going to be taken away from you. And then the strike."

The season-ending strike meant that Chipper would have to wait anxiously until the following spring to see whether his knee would allow him to play baseball in the same way that he had before the injury. He had always relied on his speed to steal bases and run down balls that seemed out of reach. "I never wondered whether I was going to be back," he said. "What I worried about was whether the old Chipper Jones would be back. The guy who had the speed to steal 25 bases, the guy who could turn doubles into triples."

What Chipper was wondering about, really, was whether

he'd lost his opportunity to bring his full package to Atlanta. "Before I got hurt, I didn't feel like I had any weakness in my game," said Chipper, who had to spend the winter wondering whether he'd ever be the complete ball player that he had been before the injury.

5. Rookie

In 1995, the preseason was compressed into only 11 games, from the usual 30 or so, because the squabbling owners and players took that long to even *tentatively* resolve the collective bargaining dispute that had brought the game to a standstill the previous August. Chipper was rusty from his 18-month layoff from competition and was forced to learn how to play third base, a new position for him. He hit only .241 during the abbreviated exhibition schedule.

His work at the plate and his play in the field was so shaky that some of his teammates openly questioned Chipper's ability to even stay in the league. "I've seen plenty of players with hype who never did anything," said Atlanta rightfielder David Justice, who may have been upset by the fact that Chipper was replacing the popular Terry Pendleton at the hot corner. "It's going to be real tough year for Chipper. There's a lot of pressure playing third base in this league. With that kind of pressure. . . the next thing you know, you don't see Chipper Jones any more."

What Justice didn't realize was that Chipper had been raised in a pressure-cooker atmosphere and wasn't about to fade from the scene. Despite a shaky start both at bat and in the field, Chipper showed that he wouldn't buckle under the dual weight of being a rookie *and* learning a new position at the major league level. "Look," Chipper explained. "I worked my butt off to get here. I'm going to work even harder to stay here."

And, when the team limped through early June five games out of first place, Chipper showed that he could take the heat of publicly challenging his veteran teammates. "We need a kick in the rear," he told reporters. "We need some vocal leaders on this team. We're not doing the little things it takes to win. This has got to stop!"

The veterans were shocked to hear a rookie talking like this. Some of them were furious with Chipper and yelled at him, but he didn't back off. "Chipper's no rookie," said veteran teammate Tom Glavine. "He came in here a very mature player. He knows exactly what he is saying and doing."

Chipper's words definitely seemed to have an effect on his teammates, who went on to win 22 of their next 31 games. By July 5, they had taken over first place in the NL East and went on to take the divisional title by an astounding 21 games.

Chipper reminded a lot of baseball people of players from a different generation. They looked at him and saw the type of player who played in the 1950s and 1960s, players like Mickey Mantle, Jackie Robinson, and Willie Mays.

"He would have fit right in," said Cox, whose professional career began in 1950. "Chipper reminds you of those guys. He plays the game the way it was played back then. He's a gutty guy who knows the game."

"If people want to call me a throwback [to that era], that's as flattering a thing as anybody can say about me," declared Chipper. "Back then, people didn't play for money. They played for the love of the game. They played to win championships and build dynasties. That was a tremendously competitive era, and I would have loved to experience that."

How different is it today?

"Today, some guys play for the wrong reasons," he said. "They play for the love of $40 million. If I ever got to feeling that way, you'll know it, because it will be the day I quit."

Jones is especially proud when people compare him to Mickey Mantle. "Whenever guys say I remind them of Mickey Mantle, that's the ultimate compliment. He was my idol and he was my father's idol," said Chipper, who even dresses like players from the 1950s. Although almost all current players wear their pants down to their shoes, Chipper wears his dark blue sox high, all the way up his calf, just like Mickey Mantle did.

Chipper finished his rookie season hitting .265, with 23 homers and 86 RBIs. Although those were fine numbers for a first-year player, Chipper was a little disappointed. "I feel like I'm a .300 hitter in this league," he said. "I expected more of myself."

Although he hadn't played up to his own high level of expectation, his manager was completely satisfied with Chipper's progress. "Chipper is already one of the best third basemen in the league," insisted Cox, despite the fact that Chipper made 25 errors, the third highest total among major league third basemen. "You have to remember that this guy was a shortstop. He got only 11 games in spring training and he had been out for 18 months before. He really came on well for us."

In the postseason, Chipper elevated his game to an even higher level, starting with Atlanta's three-game sweep over the Colorado Rockies in the National League Divisional Series.

In Game 1, Chipper hit two homers, including the game-winner with two outs in the top of the ninth inning. He also made a game-saving catch in the eighth inning, when he dove and stabbed a line drive that was heading down the left field line.

Chipper also came up big in Game 2, starting the game-tying rally in the ninth inning and the game-winning rally in the 11th. And, in Game 3, the series clincher, Chipper knocked in two runs with a double.

He finished the series hitting .389, with two doubles, two homers and four RBIs.

Chipper continued his hot streak, batting .438 in the Atlanta's four-game sweep of the Cincinnati Reds in the National League Championship Series.

In Game 1, with Atlanta trailing by one in the ninth, Chipper led off the inning with a single and came around to score the tying run.

In Game 3, with Atlanta holding onto a slim 3–2 margin, Chipper blasted a two-run homer to break the game open.

"When I hit that home run I don't think there was a dry eye in my family," said Chipper, whose wife, parents, and grandparents were in the stands, rooting him on. "My dad must have been extra proud."

When Atlanta beat the Reds, 6–0, to complete the sweep, there was a huge victory party in the winner's locker room. Chipper, though, went outside the locker room to look for his father. When he saw Larry standing there, he said, "Dad, I don't believe it. I'm going to the World Series!!!"

In the World Series, Atlanta faced the Cleveland Indians, who were easily the class of the American League, with an All-Star at virtually every position.

Nobody, though, was going to get in the way of Atlanta, who won the series, four games to two, and gave the city the first hometown champion in its entire professional sports history.

Chipper showed a mature understanding of how special it was to be on a World Series winner. "I know that some very good players go through their entire careers and never get this opportunity," he said. "So I feel very fortunate. I don't feel *lucky*, because I've worked awfully hard to get here, but I definitely feel fortunate. The only thing that's been a little bit of a surprise to me is how relaxed I was before each game. I thought I'd be more nervous. But I've been through a lot of pressure games in my life. Some guys live for crunch time. I'm one of them."

When the season was over, most people expected Chipper to be named the National League's Rookie of the Year by the Baseball Writers of America. Instead, the award went to Los Angeles Dodgers pitcher Hideo Nomo, who also had a terrific season, going 13–6, with a 2.54 ERA and 236 strikeouts in just 191.1 innings.

"But I got the grand prize," noted Chipper. "I won the World Series and they can never take that away from me. Hopefully, one of these days, I'll be in the running for the Most Valuable Player Award, or something like that."

And Chipper was named the *Sporting News* Rookie of the Year. Although this isn't as prestigious as the Baseball Writers' award, it meant more to him because it is voted on by major league players.

6. Sophomore Jinx?

Chipper was in especially good spirits when he reported to Atlanta's spring training site in West Palm Beach, Florida. He had just signed a new four-year, $8.25 million contract, which was a big boost over the $109,000 minimum wage salary that he had earned as a rookie. The length of the contract also established the fact that Atlanta general manager John Schuerholz considered Chipper to be a cornerstone of the franchise's future.

The only thing that seemed to stand in the way of Chipper having a successful 1996 season was the dreaded "Sophomore Jinx." It's something that happens all the time in the world of sports. A person has a terrific rookie season, only to do terribly in their second year. There have even been players who played like superstars as rookies and were never really heard from again.

Chipper knew all about the jinx. It was something he thought about all through the offseason between the 1995 and 1996 seasons. "There is a sophomore jinx," he said. "But it happens only if you let it happen. Guys who are content with their rookie year, who go home and don't work out, who come to camp lackadaisical, it happens to *them*."

That's certainly not the way Chipper approached his offseason. He spent the winter running, lifting weights, and adding 20 pounds of muscle to his 6–3 frame. He also worked out on the ball field, taking thousands of ground balls to improve his defense, and hitting hundreds and hundreds of pitches to keep his batting eye sharp. But Chipper's extensive offseason work seemed pointless when he arrived at camp and discovered that he needed more surgery on his right knee. Luckily, though, the operation was only a minor one, and Chipper was back in the starting lineup for the fifth game of the 1996 season.

Chipper's main goal for the season was to improve his hitting. He was not at all happy with his .265 average as a rookie. He had never hit that badly over a full season in his life and he didn't intend to allow himself to be a mediocre major leaguer.

During the early going, though, Chipper appeared to be treading water. He finished the month of April hitting only .261. "My timing was really off," he said. "My bat speed slowed down while I was out with the knee. I was getting beat on pitches and I really struggled. Luckily, I finally got in the groove," he added, "There's a big difference in the way I'm hitting this year" "I got caught up in trying to hit the long ball too much last year. Now, when pitchers pitch me away, I'm taking the ball out that way instead of always trying to pull it. I'm hitting for a higher average, but I'm also getting more opposite-field homers."

June was better, as Chipper's average rose to .309. Even more remarkably, he was putting up some impressive power numbers as well. By the end of the month, he already had 15 homers and 62 RBIs.

The first half of his season was so outstanding that he was selected to play in the 1996 All-Star Game. When Chipper walked onto the field at Philadelphia's Veterans Stadium, he was dazzled by the array of future Hall of Famers, such as Bobby Bonds, Tony Gwynn, Cal Ripen, and Wade Boggs. He was most in awe, though, of St. Louis Cardinals shortstop Ozzie Smith, the Wizard of Oz, who was finishing off the final season in a career that has earned him consideration as the best shortstop in the history of the game.

"It was really like a dream," Chipper said. "I looked over and was playing beside Ozzie Smith. This guy had been in 14 All-Star games. It was an honor for me to be playing with him. Hopefully, in 15 years, it will be my 14th All-Star Game. That's what I'm going to shoot for."

After the All-Star Game, Chipper simply picked up where he had left off. By the end of August, he had raised his batting average to .316, and upped his homer count to 29 and his RBI total to 102. Although his hitting tailed off in September, Chipper ended the season among the league leaders in the major offensive categories. More important than the numbers—a .309 batting average, 30 homers, and 110 RBI—Chipper had established himself as the most valuable everyday player on the winningest team in baseball.

Having played so well throughout the 1995 playoffs, Chipper was expecting only good things in the 1996 playoffs, despite the fact that he was weakened by a flu bug. As it turned out, though, Chipper's teammates had to carry him to a pair of wins over the Los Angeles Dodgers in the National League Division Series.

The first game turned out to be a terrific pitching duel between Atlanta's Cy Young Award winner, John Smoltz, and Ramon Martinez, with Atlanta coming out on top 2–1 in 10 innings. Atlanta also pulled out Game 2, relying on solo home runs by Fred McGriff, Ryan Klesko, and Jermaine Dye to win 3–2.

In Game 3, Chipper, who was 0–6 in the series, finally came alive. He hit a homer and a single, walked, and stole a base as Atlanta swept the Dodgers with a 5–2 win.

In the National League Championship Series, Chipper got off to a much better start, helping Atlanta to a 4–2 victory over the St. Louis Cardinals with a 4–4 performance. "I was still feeling lousy [from the flu]," Chipper said. "I didn't hit one of those balls hard, but somehow I ended up with four hits. There are games when you hit everything hard and nothing falls in, so I'll take a game like this one."

Atlanta, which had won the first four games of the 1996 playoffs, was looking invincible, especially with Greg Maddux and Tom Glavine waiting to take their turns on the mound. But St. Louis third baseman Gary Gaetti smacked a grand slam homer off Maddux, leading the Cardinals to an 8–3 victory, and the Cards followed that with a 3–2 victory over Tom Glavine.

Atlanta, looking to tie the series, held a 3–0 lead going into the bottom of the seventh in Game 4, but the Cards rallied, scoring three runs in the seventh and one in the eighth to pull out the victory and take a commanding 3–1 lead in the best-of-seven series. "Everybody was in shock," Chipper said. "Don't believe what anybody tells you, we were really worried. When you lose a game like that, you know you're in big trouble."

Atlanta didn't quit, though. In the critical fifth game, centerfielder Marquis Grissom led off the first inning for Atlanta with a single, and Mark Lemke doubled him to third. That brought up Chipper, who responded with one of the biggest hits of his career, a double down the left field line that put Atlanta up 2–0, on their way to a 14–0 victory. "That really woke us up," Chipper said. "We hadn't been hitting and, boy, that felt good."

Maddux pitched brilliantly to help Atlanta tie the series at 3–3. Then it was Glavine who came up big in Game 7, pitching seven shutout innings while his teammates pounded out a 15–0 series-clinching victory. Chipper had two singles and scored two runs in the game to finish the NLCS batting a hefty .440. "We showed a lot of character," Chipper said. "I don't care who you are playing. To come back from 3–1 in a championship series tells you a lot about our team.

"It's great to be back in the World Series. But I don't think this team will be satisfied, unless we win it all."

Atlanta's World Series foes were the New York Yankees, and Chipper couldn't have been more thrilled. This was the team Mickey Mantle had played for. Chipper had always dreamed of playing in Yankee Stadium, the most famous stadium in all of baseball. Now he would have his chance.

The series began at in New York, but Atlanta played as if they had the home field advantage. In Game 1, they crushed the Yankees 12–1. Andruw Jones gave the Braves a 2–0 lead in the first inning with a homer to right, then Chipper extended the lead to 4–0 in the second with a two-run single.

"Chipper's hit is the one that killed us," said Yankees starter Andy Pettitte. "Two-nothing is still pretty close, but 4–0 took us out of the game."

Game 2 was also a piece of cake, with Maddux pitching eight shutout innings as the visitors cruised to a 4–0 win.

The Series moved from the House that Ruth Built to Atlanta's Fulton County Stadium, a building due to be torn down as soon as the Series was over. Atlanta had to win only two of the next five games to repeat as World Series Champions, but that's not the way it worked out.

The Yankees rallied to win Game 3, and then came back from a 6–0 deficit to capture Game 4, 8–6, in 10 innings. The Yankees completed their improbable three-game sweep the following night, 1–0, as John Smoltz and Andy Pettitte locked up in a thrilling pitching duel that was decided by an unearned run. Chipper kept Atlanta's hopes alive by leading off the bottom of the ninth with a double, but John Wetteland, the Series MVP, shut the door on the home team, stranding Chipper, the potential tying run, at third base.

The Yankees jumped out to an early 3–0 lead in Game 6, but Atlanta shaved the margin to 3–2. In the ninth inning, Atlanta had two men out and two on base, with Mark Lemke facing Wetteland and Chipper kneeling in the on-deck circle, hoping for a chance to be a hero.

But as Chipper choked his bat handle, Wetteland smoked a 3–2 fastball that handcuffed Lemke, forcing him into hitting a harmless pop foul that Yankee third baseman Charlie Hayes squeezed into his glove for the final out of the 1996 World Series.

"I was just sort of numb," said Chipper, who never got the chance to deliver the crucial hit and watched as the Yankees celebrated. "You've got to give them credit. They could have folded their tents after the first two games, but they came into our place and whipped on us pretty good. That takes a lot of guts, a lot of heart."

Chipper also had trouble accepting his own numbers in the World Series. His average, .286, wasn't terrible, but it wasn't great either. After blasting 30 homers and knocking in 110 runs during the regular season, he had no homers and only three RBI in the World Series.

"I'll tell you something," Chipper said. "This leaves a real bitter taste in my mouth. It's going to stay there all winter. We're the winningest team in the 1990s, but we have only one World Series Championship to show for it. That's real tough to accept."

7. The Future is Bright

After only two years, Chipper has established himself as an All-Star and a champion. Don't expect him to rest on his laurels, though. As impressive as his numbers were in 1996, they weren't nearly where Chipper thinks they could be—where he expects them to be.

"I'm a bit of a perfectionist," he said. "I'm always picking at what's wrong and trying to correct it so my game will be flawless. I'm looking for that point in my game where I'm hitting .300 from both sides of the plate with power, I'm driving the ball, and I'm playing flawless defense. That's not happening yet."

Although his fielding improved from 1995 to 1996, Chipper knows that there's much more room for improvement. He wants to be the National League's Gold Glove winner, year after year, at third base.

There are other goals that Chipper has yet to reach. He wants to match Ozzie Smith's record of 14 All-Star Games. He wants to win the National League's MVP, at least once. Winning one World Series was nice, but not nearly enough.

"I've got only one [World Series] ring," he said. "And I've got nine more fingers. Actually, make that eight fingers. I've got my wedding ring on."

Although Chipper is dissatisfied with his production thus far, he's not at all unhappy. He has a great life with his wife, Karin. They are building a huge home in Atlanta and they are planning to have children soon.

Chipper does miss his privacy, though. He has become so popular in Atlanta that he can't even go to a movie or a restaurant without being swarmed by people.

Even when he stays home, fans make their way to his lawn, just camping out, hoping to get a glimpse of their favorite player. "Fans go way too far," he said. "I don't mind them asking for autographs and stuff at the stadium, but not when I'm home. That's a little tough for me and Karin."

Nevertheless, Chipper knows that the personal inconvenience is a relatively small price to pay for where he's at. "I'm playing a game for a living," he marveled. "That's fun in itself. The fact that I'm playing for the best organization in baseball makes it that much more fun. I'm contributing individually and I'm putting up some numbers that are being recognized around the rest of the league. How can I not be having fun?"

With all his success, Chipper doesn't forget what got him to this point. He remembers the things he learned from his parents, the encouragement they gave him, and the endless hours he spent with his dad practicing his hitting, pitching, and fielding.

To this day, he can close his eyes and see himself as Mickey Mantle, with his father pitching him a whiffle ball.

"I've definitely been blessed with a whole lot of talent," he said. "That, I can thank God for. I can also thank Him for giving me parents who instilled a strong work ethic.

"There are a whole lot of guys who have talent. The ones who make it are the ones who work at it."

If you want to write to the author, address your letter to:

Jon Gelberg
4 Tanglewood Road
North Caldwell NJ 07006

If you want to write to the players, address your letters to:

Mark McGwire
c/o The Oakland A's
7767 Oakport Street
2nd Floor
Oakland CA 94621

Chipper Jones
c/o The Atlanta Braves
P.O. Box 4064
Atlanta GA 30302

If you want to write a letter complaining about team nicknames and logos, you may write to individual teams and/or to the commissioners. Address your letter to:

Baseball Commissioner's Office
Major League Baseball
350 Park Avenue
NY NY 10022

Commissioner Pete Tagliabue
c/o NFL
410 Park Avenue
NY NY 10022

Cleveland Baseball Team
Jacobs Field
2401 Ontario Street
Cleveland OH 44115

Washington NFL Football Team
21300 Redskin Park Drive
Ashburn VA 22011

Sources

The Atlanta Journal-Constitution

Atlanta Magazine

Baseball Weekly

The Chicago Tribune

The Kansas City Star

The Los Angeles Times

Newsday

The New York Times

The Orlando Sentinel

The St. Petersburg Times

The San Francisco Chronicle

The Sporting News

Sports Illustrated

The Tampa Tribune

USA Today

MARK MCGWIRE

Birthdate: October 1, 1963 Birthplace: Pomona, California
Height: 6'-5" Weight: 240
Bats: R Throws: R

Career Record

Year	Club	G	AB	R	H	2B	3B	HR	RBIs	BB	SO	SB	AVE
86	Oak	18	53	10	10	1	0	3	9	4	18	0	.189
87	Oak	151	557	97	161	28	4	49	118	71	131	1	.289
88	Oak	155	550	87	143	22	1	32	99	76	117	1	.260
89	Oak	143	490	74	113	17	0	33	95	83	94	1	.231
90	Oak	156	523	87	123	16	0	39	108	110	116	2	.235
91	Oak	154	483	62	97	22	0	22	75	93	116	2	.201
92	Oak	139	467	87	125	22	0	42	104	90	105	0	.268
93	Oak	27	84	16	28	6	0	9	24	21	19	0	.333
94	Oak	47	135	26	34	3	0	9	25	37	40	0	.252
95	Oak	104	317	75	87	13	0	39	90	88	77	1	.274
96	Oak	130	423	104	132	21	0	52	113	116	112	0	.312
ML Totals		1224	4082	725	1053	171	5	329	860	789	945	7	.258

ALCS

Year	Club	G	AB	R	H	2B	3B	HR	RBIs	BB	SO	SB	AVE
88	Oak	4	15	4	5	0	0	1	3	1	5	0	.333
89	Oak	5	18	3	7	1	0	1	3	1	4	0	.389
90	Oak	4	13	2	2	0	0	0	2	3	3	0	.154
92	Oak	6	20	1	3	0	0	1	3	5	4	0	.150
Totals		19	66	10	17	1	0	3	11	10	16	0	.258

World Series

Year	Club	G	AB	R	H	2B	3B	HR	RBIs	BB	SO	SB	AVE
88	Oak	5	17	1	1	0	0	1	1	3	4	0	.059
89	Oak	4	17	0	5	1	0	0	1	1	3	0	.294
90	Oak	4	14	1	3	0	0	0	0	2	4	0	.214
Totals		13	48	2	9	1	0	1	2	6	11	0	.188

CHIPPER JONES

Birthdate: April 24, 1972   **Birthplace:** Deland, Florida
Height: 6'3"   **Weight:** 200
Bats: R &L   **Throws:** R

Year	Club	G	AB	R	H	2B	3B	HR	RBIs	BB	SO	SB	AVE
90	Bradenton	44	140	20	32	1	1	1	18	14	25	5	.229
91	Macon	163	473	104	154	24	11	15	98	69	70	40	.326
92	Durham	70	264	43	73	22	1	4	31	31	34	10	.277
92	Greenville	67	266	43	92	17	11	9	42	11	32	14	.346
93	Richmond	139	536	97	174	31	12	13	89	57	70	23	.325
93	Atlanta	8	3	2	2	1	0	0	0	1	1	0	.667
94	Atlanta	On Disabled List											
95	Atlanta	140	524	87	139	22	3	23	86	73	99	8	.265
96	Atlanta	157	598	114	185	32	5	30	110	87	88	14	.309
ML Totals		305	1125	203	326	55	8	53	196	161	188	22	.290

Division Series

		G	AB	R	H	2B	3B	HR	RBIs	BB	SO	SB	AVE
95 vs. Col.		4	18	4	7	2	0	2	4	2	2	0	.389
96 vs. LA		3	9	2	2	0	0	1	2	1	1	0	.222
Totals		7	27	6	9	2	0	3	6	3	3	0	.333

NLCS

		G	AB	R	H	2B	3B	HR	RBIs	BB	SO	SB	AVE
95 vs. Cin.		4	16	3	7	0	0	1	3	3	1	1	.438
96 vs. St. L		7	25	6	11	2	0	0	4	3	1	1	.440
Totals		11	41	9	18	2	0	1	7	6	2	2	.439

World Series

		G	AB	R	H	2B	3B	HR	RBIs	BB	SO	SB	AVE
95 vs. Cle		6	21	3	6	3	0	0	1	4	3	0	.286
96 vs. NYY		6	21	3	6	3	0	0	3	4	2	1	.286
Totals		12	42	6	12	6	0	0	4	8	5	1	.286

If you enjoyed this book, you might want to order some of our other exciting titles:

BASKETBALL SUPERSTARS ALBUM 1996, Richard J. Brenner. Includes 16 full-color pages, and mini-bios of the game's top superstars, plus career and all-time stats. 48 pages.

MICHAEL JORDAN * MAGIC JOHNSON, by Richard J. Brenner. A dual biography of two of the greatest superstars of all time. 128 pages, 15 dynamite photos.

ANFERNEE HARDAWAY * GRANT HILL, by Brian Cazeneuve. A dual biography of two of the brightest young stars in basketball. 96 pages, 10 pages of photos.

SHAQUILLE O'NEAL * LARRY JOHNSON, by Richard J. Brenner. A dual biography of two of the brightest young stars in basketball. 96 pages, 10 pages of photos.

PRO FOOTBALL'S ALL-TIME ALL-STAR TEAM   , by Richard J. Brenner. The top 24 football players of all time are profiled in this photo-filled book. 128 pages.

STEVE YOUNG * JERRY RICE, by Richard J. Brenner. A dual biography of the two superstars who led the 49ers to the Super Bowl. 96 pages, 10 pages of photos.

TROY AIKMAN * STEVE YOUNG, by Richard J. Brenner. A dual biography of the top two quarterbacks in the NFL. 96 pages, 10 pages of photos.

GREG MADDUX * CAL RIPKEN, JR., by Richard J. Brenner. A dual biography of two future Hall of Famers. 96 pages, 10 pages of photos.

KEN GRIFFEY JR. * FRANK THOMAS, by Brian Cazeneuve. A dual biography of two of baseball's brightest young superstars. 96 pages, 10 pages of photos.

MARIO LEMIEUX, by Richard J. Brenner. An exciting biography of one of hockey's all-time greats. 96 pages, 10 pages of photos.

THE WORLD SERIES, THE GREAT CONTESTS, by Richard J. Brenner. The special excitement of the Fall Classic is brought to life through seven of the most thrilling Series ever played, including 1993. 176 pages, including 16 action-packed photos.

MICHAEL JORDAN, by Richard J. Brenner. An easy-to-read, photo-filled biography especially for younger readers. 32 pages.

GRANT HILL, by Richard J. Brenner. An easy-to-read, photo-filled biography especially for younger readers. 32 pages.

SHAQUILLE O'NEAL, by Richard J. Brenner. An easy-to-read, photo-filled biography especially for younger readers. 32 pages.

WAYNE GRETZKY, by Richard J. Brenner. An easy-to-read, photo-filled biography especially for younger readers. 32 pages.

TOUCHDOWN! THE FOOTBALL FUN BOOK, by Richard J. Brenner. Trivia, puzzles, mazes and much more! 64 pages.

PLEASE SEE NEXT PAGE FOR ORDER FORM

ORDER FORM

Payment must accompany all orders and must be in U.S. dollars.

Postage and handling is $1.35 per book up to a maximum of $6.75 ($1.75 to a maximum of $8.75 in Canada).

Mr. Brenner will personally autograph his books for an additional cost of $1.00 per book.

Please send me the following books:

No. of copies	Title	Price
_____	BASKETBALL SUPERSTARS ALBUM 1996	$4.50/$6.25 Can.
_____	MICHAEL JORDAN * MAGIC JOHNSON	$3.50/$4.25 Can.
_____	ANFERNEE HARDAWAY * GRANT HILL	$3.99/$5.50 Can.
_____	SHAQUILLE O'NEAL * LARRY JOHNSON	$3.50/$4.50 Can.
_____	PRO FOOTBALL'S ALL-TIME ALL-STAR TEAM	$4.50/$5.50 Can.
_____	DEION SANDERS*BRETT FAVRE	$3.99/$5.50 Can.
_____	STEVE YOUNG * JERRY RICE	$3.99/$5.50 Can.
_____	TROY AIKMAN * STEVE YOUNG	$3.50/$4.50 Can.
_____	GREG MADDUX * CAL RIPKEN, JR.	$3.99/$5.50 Can.
_____	KEN GRIFFEY JR. * FRANK THOMAS	$3.50/$4.50 Can.
_____	MARIO LEMIEUX	$3.50/$4.50 Can.
_____	THE WORLD SERIES, THE GREAT CONTESTS	$4.50/$5.50 Can.
_____	MICHAEL JORDAN	$4.00/$5.50 Can.
_____	GRANT HILL	$3.50/$4.50 Can.
_____	SHAQUILLE O'NEAL	$3.25/$4.50 Can.
_____	WAYNE GRETZKY	$3.25/$4.50 Can.
_____	TOUCHDOWN! THE FOOTBALL FUN BOOK	$3.50/$5.00 Can.

TOTAL NUMBER OF BOOKS ORDERED   _____

TOTAL PRICE OF BOOKS $_____

POSTAGE AND HANDLING $_____

AUTOGRAPHING COST $_____

TOTAL PAYMENT ENCLOSED $_____

NAME _____

ADDRESS _____

CITY _____ STATE _____ ZIP _____ COUNTRY _____

Send to: East End Publishing, 54 Alexander Drive, Syosset NY 11791 USA. Dept. TD. Allow three weeks for delivery. Discounts are available on orders of 25 or more copies. For details call (516) 364-6383.